Electric Strawberry

Alexis Roy

BookLeaf Publishing

Presentation by *BookLeaf Publishing*

Web: www.bookleafpub.com

E-mail: info@bookleafpub.com

ISBN: 9789357445986

First edition 2023

To Drew, Oliver and Stanley. Thank you for being my world xxx

Comedy

Life of a comic
Self-loathing and elation
Irresistible

Motherhood

Overwhelmed.
They don't tell you that's how you'll feel
The chaos, the frenzy, the relentlessness

Tired.
They don't tell you how tired you'll be
How you'll yearn for sleep like a forbidden drug

Snappy.
You'll lose it over the smallest things
Your patience worn down when your tank is empty

But.

Love.
You'll feel a love greater than ever
Your heart will burst when you see them smile at you
They look up to you now and never
Forget that the hard times make the good times true

To Mum

When you passed away, all hope was lost
Your love and light and laughter dimmed
How to live in an eternal frost
Where sun and warmth have died within

Your life was full of love and charm
A life lived with hope, intent and grace
But when you left, we lost that calm
And now I cannot see your face

So time is meant to heal the pain
We learn to live without you here
But pain endures time and again
It hurts more than it did last year

The sun shines on the sea when I think of you
And as I try to live on,I hope you can see me
too.

I am a mum

Both laughing, crying,
Learning, surviving each day
I am a mother

Learning to say no

Week in week out, the schedules running
repeatedly with routine
The hamster wheel, I can't get off, how to say
no.
There is no end, no break from the endless list of
tasks
Round and round the clock hands go; I am no
further forward.

Time goes on with quickening speed, yet
nothing seems to change
The diaries, always blocked, how to make the
space.
How can time go so fast and yet everything
stand still.
On and on the calendar moves; I cannot seem to
breathe.

Learn to put the boundaries in, I need to know
when to say no
I cannot be everywhere, for everyone and still be
me
I must be strong, I must be confident in pushing
back
To be present and happy, I need to value my
time.

Sadness

At my lowest ebb
The waves crashing on the jagged rocks
My mood a boat being tossed about in the sea
I am low
But I will rise again.
I am a fighter.
The storm will pass.

My sons

Always making noise
Always eating many snacks
I will always love you, boys.

Self

Understanding me
Such a high mountain to climb
But i will get there.

Sorry

Sorry to the younger me
Who sat alone at school
The girl who found it hard you see
The words of others were cruel

I forced you to be false with them
I made you pretend to be
Someone who you simply weren't
Because I wanted to be happy

I'm sorry I didn't listen
I'm sorry I didn't help
We will get through this together.

We will be ourselves.

Time

Time ticks by so slow
And yet it goes by so fast
Please make it stand still.

Normal

Is it normal, I ask myself
Should I be this sad
Should I be the one to help
My dysfunctional dad

He used to be my guiding light
The one to make me laugh
And now all we do is fight
We are on completely different paths

I want us to be friends again
But I cannot see how we can
You brought about the eternal rain
And all I feel is sad.

Winter

Icy, cold, frosty
White frozen pavements, chilly
Sat next to the fire

The future

I hate how I look
I hate how I sound
I hate how I think, feel and behave.
One day I will be happy
Content
At peace

That day is coming.

Rain

Dropping on the roof
Soporific dripping sounds
Truly magical.

Sleep tight

I watch you sleep, I love you
Your little face as it sleeps soundly
Your breath
Your nose
Your eyes
The eyelashes as they twitch in your sleep
I will watch you and love you until the end of time

Dog

There once was a dog called Snoot
Who had a nose like a boot
He enjoyed eating carrots
And loved chasing parrots
And running outside was a hoot.

Summer

Sun, beating downwards
It takes my breath away
Brught, warm on my skin.

Autumn

Leaves on the hard ground
Golden, brown and red, gorgeous
The trees are glowing.

Spring

Flowers and bluebells
The sound of birds in the trees
It's spectacular.

Grief

It never leaves you
The empty feeling of grief
You learn to exist.

I am

I am me
Bold and bright and big and loud
I will no longer be the pleaser
The one who runs and runs to make people happy
I am me
And that's great.
I'm proud to be me.

www.ingramcontent.com/pod-product-compliance
Lightning Source LLC
Chambersburg PA
CBHW051721130826
49812CB00034B/1290
9789357445986